OVER
100
WAYS TO
LEAVE YOUR
LOVER
AND BE HAPPIER
THAN EVER

THIS IS A CARLTON BOOK

Text, illustrations and design copyright © 2002 Carlton Books Limited

This edition published by
Carlton Books Limited 2002
20 Mortimer Street
London W1T 3JW

A CIP catalogue record for this book is available from the British Library
ISBN 1 84222 501 4

Printed and bound in Malaysia

Art Director: Penny Stock
Senior Art Editor: Barbara Zuñiga
Executive Editor: Zia Mattocks
Design: DW Design
Editor: Lisa Dyer
Production Manager: Garry Lewis
Illustrator: Robert Loxston

COSMOPOLITAN

OVER 100 WAYS TO LEAVE YOUR LOVER

AND BE HAPPIER THAN EVER

LISA SUSSMAN

CARLTON BOOKS

Section One

Denial

this isn't happening to me

Studies have found that it doesn't matter if you are the dumper or dumpee – EVERYONE has to go through emotional phases similar to grieving in order to deal with relationship meltdown.

The first stage is denial. As in, 'Huh? I didn't see it coming. OK, things haven't been working out for a while, but it's not like he's an axe murderer.'

The reality is, unless things are blatantly bad – he's hitting you, cheating on you with everything on the planet, wearing your clothes – it can be hard to be 100 per cent positive that this guy isn't your Mr Right. Even then, you may think, 'Maybe this is just a rough spot that we need to work through,' or, 'It's me – I'll change and things will get better.' Odds are, once you're feeling this way, they won't. Here's how to tell where to draw the line.

OVER AND OUT

Swift ways to figure out if he's the real deal
or if the two of you are history:

You're starting to **abhor** what you
used to **adore**. A University of Ohio
study found that there's a flip side
to love in that the things that first
attract us are often the very things
that start turning us off when the
relationship is skidding towards a
dead end. So his sexy take-charge
attitude now seems controlling. Your
fun-loving 'life of the party' suddenly
seems more like an odious flirt. And
his charming romantic streak begins
to feel needy and insecure.

You argue over who started
the last big fight.

3

You're putting up with behaviour from him that you wouldn't normally tolerate from a bank teller or shoe salesman, let alone someone you supposedly love. Research by relationship guru Barbara De Angelis, PhD, has found that women – especially younger ones – are easily susceptible to the myth that **Love Conquers All** and will, therefore, stay in a relationship way past its prime in the hope that the man will (miraculously) change (see tips 15–19 for other bogus true romance beliefs).

Love him/Dump him

- You have good sex together regularly/ The only thing that's good about being together is the regular sex.
- He's yours/He's there.
- Looking at him, you think, 'How did I get so lucky?'/Looking at him, you wonder, 'WHAT was I thinking?'
- You know no-one will ever love you like he does/You fear no-one will ever ask you out again.
- His screensaver is a picture of you/His screensaver is a picture of a naked woman (not you).

5

A man from your past shows up
and, even though he's straight
out of jail, you don't hesitate
to straddle his Harley.

6

You don't panic that he may be
flirting with his new assistant
at work (the one you know
for a fact is an ex-porn star).

7

You hate the way he breathes.

DON'T GET BURNED

Seven secret signs your man is about to bolt:

8

He's been criticizing you big time. According to communication experts, this is the typical male way of saying, 'I'm not really interested in you anymore,' while justifying his decision to bail. His secret wish? That you'll get so fed up, you'll say, 'I'm outta here.'

He introduces you as his **'friend'**.

10

He asks you if you have ever thought about **having an affair** (translation: HE's thinking about it).

He suddenly starts making nice with you. According to a Texas Christian University study, there's a break-up blueprint that most people follow when they're getting ready to dissolve their partnership: you notice other people, you guiltily try to make things lovey-dovey with your own partner, you get pissed off with the effort, repeat the cycle twice and then call it quits.

11

You notice a dramatic **shift in your sex life**. If you did it a lot, you now do it less, and vice versa. An Archives of Sexual Behaviour study discovered that the former happens because he's getting it elsewhere (or fantasizing about it); and the latter because he is desperately trying to make things work out.

He suggests a repeat performance of that time you had amazing **sex in the lift** (elevator) – only you've never had sex in a lift.

He won't make plans for the future, even for tomorrow night. Research on men and communication confirms what you knew all along: guys are notorious for not breaking bad – or ANY – news. To avoid confrontation, he might stop talking, calling or e-mailing, or move to another city – anything to keep from telling you he wants out. If you do corner him, he's likely to stutter and stammer, make a joke out of it or blurt it out in a way that feels like a groin kick from Jackie Chan.

ONCE UPON A TIME

Unless you want to become the heartbreak queen, erase these love myths from your heart.

Myth: You think he is the only one.
Reality: Wrong. There are millions of potential soulmates for every person in the world.

Myth: Your heart will never fully recover.
Reality: It will.

Myth: True love conquers all.
Reality: True love doesn't conquer a lying, cheating bastard or even a Mr Not-Quite-Right who is perfectly sweet but leaves you yawning.

Myth: 'If only I were prettier, thinner or smarter (or whatever!), it would have worked out.'
Reality: You might be Gwyneth Paltrow's more gorgeous cousin who could kick ass on the *Weakest Link* and he'll still dump you if he wants out of the relationship.

18 19

Myth: When you have incredible body-melting sex with someone, it must be love.
Reality: When you have incredible body-melting sex with someone, it must be a great orgasm.

Section Two

Bargaining

should you let him go?

All you want to know is what you can do to **stop the pain. NOW**. You have reached stage two.

Obviously, it's always better to be the leaver than the leavee. First of all, because it's going to be more of an ego boost to be the one who is doing the dumping rather than the one who is getting dumped. But also, you need to be the one to call it a day if you think you might have even a remote interest in getting your ex back sometime in the future.

A slew of studies on the perverse workings of the human mind have found that we are more likely to want what we cannot have. Ergo: leave him and you instantly become catnip for him.

So here's how to let your man know that he is about to rejoin the singles world.

THE BLOW-OFF

A clean break is all in the timing.

AFTER A FEW DATES

THE METHOD: Become the invisible woman.

HOW TO DO IT: If you've just had one date, don't answer his calls or e-mails. He'll either (a) forget about you, (b) meet someone new or (c) assume you've been kidnapped by a cult. If you've had a few more dates but aren't really a 'relationship' yet, allow so much time to pass between dates that in the interim travel agents have started selling trips to Mars. Do this by screening your calls, hanging out where he doesn't and wearing a wig in public.

KEY PHRASES: If he happens to catch you unexpectedly, simply say you're so busy right now that you don't have time for anything but work. For the truly dense, you may have to use the 'I've met someone else' line (for other options, see tips 23 and 24).

AFTER A FEW MONTHS

THE METHOD: Give him the old 'it's not you, it's me' speech. Polls show that although this is the least-used method, it's the most effective, as it keeps things from getting personal and therefore reduces the risk that he'll start hurling 'big ass' insults. That said, tip 28 also works well at this juncture.

> HOW TO DO IT: Rehearse what you are going to say in advance. This will make it easier to keep to your script and not get sidetracked into unseemly 'discussions' about the size of his genitals (you) or your eerie similarity to your mother (him). Sit him down in a public place, such as a park (he's less likely to cry, beg or get violent). Avoid restaurants and pubs (he may retaliate to your dump method by dumping food or drink over your head).

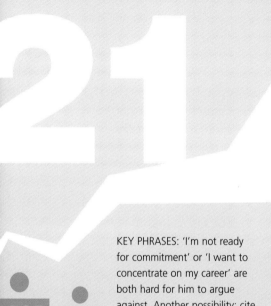

KEY PHRASES: 'I'm not ready for commitment' or 'I want to concentrate on my career' are both hard for him to argue against. Another possibility: cite irreconcilable – and, if possible, irreversible – differences, such as his religion, profession, race, height and/or country of origin.

AFTER ONE OR MORE YEARS

THE METHOD: Draw it out (but not for so long that the break-up lasts longer than the relationship itself). This way, you work through your guilt, fears of being alone and the habit of the relationship before you actually spend a night as a newly single person.

HOW TO DO IT: Have Discussions About The Relationship. Drop not-so-subtle hints about how you are losing interest. Talk about the things that really bug you (see suggestions under tip 28). Pick fights, then say, 'See? We're incompatible.' (Warning: this last one doesn't work with boyfriends in the mental health field – they'll simply call you passive-aggressive and hoodwink you into going to couples therapy.) Do this at 3 am when your defences are at their lowest.

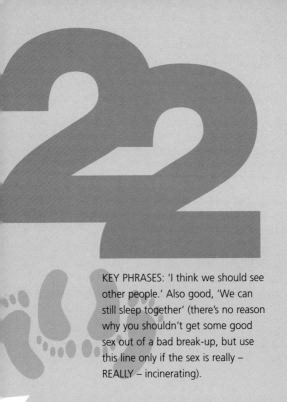

22

KEY PHRASES: 'I think we should see other people.' Also good, 'We can still sleep together' (there's no reason why you shouldn't get some good sex out of a bad break-up, but use this line only if the sex is really – REALLY – incinerating).

MAKE HIM SUFFER

According to research by Charles T Hill, PhD,
of Whittier College, California, the quickest
way to wound a guy where it hurts (read: his
babe-magnet abilities) is to dump him.

LET HIM GO GENTLY: Butter him up with more
flattery than he gets from his mother. Telling him
he's a great person who will make someone very
happy someday will make him feel so good he'll
be eager to forget you and get on with wowing
the rest of the female population.

PRICK HIM: Tell him you just want to be friends. Then offer to set him up with one of your friends, mentioning she hasn't been in a relationship for a while. He'll hear: (a) you see him as a sexless hang-out buddy, (b) who is not capable of getting his own dates and (c) is only fit for desperate women.

MAKE HIM CRY: Sleep with his best friend or brother. Remember that the best way to achieve a 'clean break' is to make it as harsh as possible, so the parties involved don't ever get to see each other again, partly due to sheer embarrassment and partly due to the restraining order.

26

SPEAK OUT

Decipher his **favourite exit lines**:

'You're much too good for me.'

Read: 'You're not the one.'

'I'm under a lot of pressure right now.'

Read: 'I don't find you sexy any more.'

'I like you too much.'

Read: 'I'm scared to get involved.'

'You're too together to put up with my crap.'

Read: 'You're boring, I'm history.'

'I'm not ready to get serious.'

Read: 'I am but not with you.'

If he has audacity to break up with you, sock it to him with these **survivor lines**:

'Phew. Now I don't have to confess about the affair I've been having.'

'Cool. I just met a hot guy and was wondering how to break it to you.'

'So now would not be a good time to tell you I've decided to become a lesbian?'

'Guess I won't be giving you that secret Eastern oral sex technique I learned as a surprise for your birthday.'

'Tell the truth – you're doing this because you feel bad that you've never been able to give me an orgasm, right?'

These **sneaky break-off tactics** are so devious,
he'll think the break-up was HIS idea (poor fool).

- One night in bed, after a particularly hot-and-heavy
  session, murmur in his ear, 'I've always wanted five
  kids – what about you?'
- Pick, pick, pick on your soon-to-be ex-lover until
  he can't wait to leave.
- Become impossibly demanding, selfish and
  possessive until he loses all interest.
- Smother your partner with love – call him ten times
  a day, insist on spending every waking moment
  with him, and tell him he is your life. He'll be
  gone before you can say, 'You complete me.'
- Tell him that you have decided to become a
  born-again virgin and plan to hold off on sex
  until you get married.
- Get caught with your pants down (see tip 25,
  Make Him Cry).

BREAKING UP IS HARD TO DO

If you're too chicken to say the words yourself, try one of these ready-made aids.

Send a card that 'bulls-eyes' your I-love-you-not message. Simply handwrite a personalized message and on-line greeting card company
www.sparks.com
will send it for you via regular old snail mail or e-mail. For those who prefer the cut-and-dried method, try this message: 'Although our lives have only crossed each other's paths for a short period of time, I can already tell you this … it's been long enough.'

When you want to avoid that I-wish-I-said-that feeling, log onto the Cyrano website at
www.nando.net/toys/cyrano.html
They'll write a personalized goodbye for you based on information you type in. Easy-peasy.

If the indirect approach is more your style, send an **anonymous note** and a trial-size bug repellent through the post, direct to his door.

If Romeo needs things spelled out more clearly, visit **www.dfilm.com**, where you can single-handedly produce a digital, animated short staging your break-up scenario, complete with soundtrack.

Tell your boyfriend **you have to talk**. Then put on Paul Simon's 'Fifty Ways To Leave Your Lover', Carol King's 'It's Too Late' or Nancy Sinatra's 'These Boots Were Made For Walking' and walk out the door.

33

Say, **'You'll be needing this'** and give him one of Melissa Etheridge's early CDs.

34

Section Three

Depression

I can't believe this is happening to me

You've just entered Splitsville (population: you). And it hurts bad, even if you were the one who downsized him.

That's because breaking up is more than just saying goodbye. It's easy to delete his number from your speed dial; it's a lot harder to get him out of your heart. Researchers at the Medical College of Virginia have found that no matter who dumped who, your likelihood of depression rises 1,130 per cent after the end up of a relationship. Hello, stage three!

Bottom line: recovery isn't going to happen overnight. Truly getting over someone takes effort. Here's your plan for getting him off your mind – and having a little fun at the same time.

TOTAL REBOUND

Follow this guide to help you dry your tears, lighten your heart and survive the first 24 hours.

35 All you want to do is **sit alone** on the floor with a candle burning and Toni Braxton wailing 'You Break My Heart' on the stereo. So go ahead – brood over him, linger over every detail of the relationship. Many people ignore or deny their pain, pretending they're doing fine. Big mistake. Psychologists have found that you need to give in to your misery now, so the feelings don't drag on and on and invade every future relationship you have with other guys, with your friends, or even with yourself (see tips 39 and 52 if you need help getting in the mood).

36 **Weep**. Snivel. Blubber. According to an Oklahoma University Health Science Center study, crying lowers blood pressure and relaxes muscles, making it a great natural tranquilliser for reducing physical and emotional agitation. But only if you tell someone about your sorrow as soon as your tears have dried (see tips 64–71 for who to call).

Take heart: the more you hurt, the better a person you are. One study found that it's the truly 'good' people – trusting, vulnerable and loving souls – who are the ones that really hurt when a relationship ends. Another upside – these are also the people who get a lot more out of life than the people who claim they've never had their heart broken.

Take out your calendar and **choose a date** to end the pity party and pull yourself together. Research has confirmed that you need to set a deadline to your emotional torment before getting on with repairing your heart (skip down to the Fix Your Heart – Fast section, tips 45–76, for some quick remedies).

Take the **sad song** cure. Play Sade, The Smiths, Alanis Morissette – any music that gives the illusion that the whole world understands how you feel right now.

As for 'your song', **avoid sobbing** whenever you hear it by giving the song a new memory. Play the song with some good friends and dance on tables, stand on your heads – do anything that will make you burst out laughing the next time you hear it.

Throw an Ex Party. Rule out anyone handing out 'you'd feel better if you got out of bed' advice (you won't). You want sympathetic souls who will listen to you endlessly recount every detail of the break-up. Let them dole out tissues and cookies, tell you you're right, that you're not getting stress zits, remind you that you're a totally smart, fab babe and give you shoulder rubs (all that tension from crying!).

Don't call him. No ifs, ands or buts. Even if you broke up with him. If he calls you, don't pick up. Studies have found you need at least a one-week breather before sane talk is even possible.

43

Use cucumber slices or cold teabags to reduce the puffiness around your eyes. Drink lots of water – it will make you feel less dehydrated after crying.

44

Do not – **DO NOT** – phone him. Especially after drinking five Cosmopolitans. Set all your speed dials to your best friend so if you do try and call him, you'll end up ringing her (she can then remind you that it's over and you are way too good for him).

FIX YOUR HEART – FAST

Follow these tips to learn how to bounce back and jump-start your life (and heart) again.

Focus on today. Take things one step at a time, one day at a time. Relationship experts say that if you start looking towards or thinking about next week, next month or next year, you'll feel overwhelmed.

Set aside a period of time each day for grieving. You're allowed to wallow in self-pity between, say, 7 and 7:30 every evening. If you find yourself thinking about HIM at 9:13 am, tell yourself you'll think about that during the allotted time.

Don't lie in bed all day fantasizing about the last great orgasm you had with him.

47

Adopt a pet. Experts say that interacting with pets can reduce blood pressure, increase the rate of healing and ease depression. Pet therapists use animals to help alleviate these symptoms among critically ill patients, and there's no reason why you can't get the same benefits (if it was a nasty break-up, adopt a pit bull terrier and take him for frequent walks around your ex's block).

Give yourself a pinch for every negative 'No-one will ever love me again' thought. This process is called retraining your brain. Ouch.

Give yourself one week to indulge – eat nothing, eat just Ben and Jerry's, go out and party, go on a shopping spree (with HIS credit cards), flirt with the postman, have (protected) meaningless sex. Then stop and reassess. Studies show this cooling-off period will help give you distance and perspective.

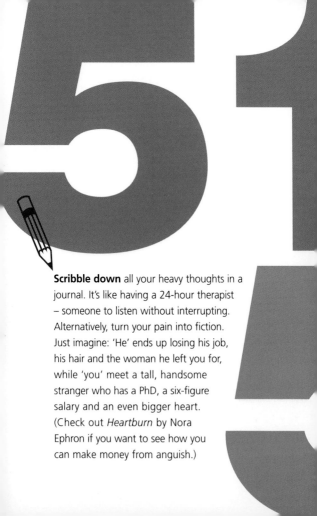

Scribble down all your heavy thoughts in a
journal. It's like having a 24-hour therapist
– someone to listen without interrupting.
Alternatively, turn your pain into fiction.
Just imagine: 'He' ends up losing his job,
his hair and the woman he left you for,
while 'you' meet a tall, handsome
stranger who has a PhD, a six-figure
salary and an even bigger heart.
(Check out *Heartburn* by Nora
Ephron if you want to see how you
can make money from anguish.)

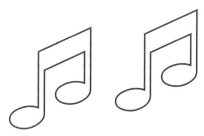

Put your pain in perspective. Listen to country music or watch a daytime talk show (in your current state of mind, you'll be able to totally relate).

53

Go on a chocolate diet. Chocolate contains a natural amphetamine, phenylethylamine, the same one our brains produce when we fall in love and that makes us feel giddy and elated. When we fall out of love, we have PEA withdrawal.

Just Do It. You probably don't much feel like breaking a sweat, but research shows that working out for just 30 minutes a day is a major mood-buster (and gut-buster if you've been following tip 53). Your body starts pumping out endorphins, those all-natural feel-good chemicals which not only kill your pain, but also make you feel inspired, strong and chock-full of self-confidence (plus you'll look fabulous if you run into him again). The added bonus: pretend the ball you're hitting, the punchbag you're slugging or the pavement you're pounding is his face.

54

Put a **positive spin** on what is happening. You may feel rejected and a failure because your relationship has disintegrated, but for every drawback there is an advantage. Don't think of it as a 'failure', but a 'transition'. You aren't 'abandoned' or 'left behind', you are 'ready for something new'. Write down all the negative statements that occur to you, and then rewrite every single one of them with a positive slant.

Call up an old friend who used to have a big-time crush on you for a little confidence-booster.

Weekends are tough for the newly single woman. Form a Saturday Night Club and have a standing date with a bunch of similarly solo friends.

Reprogram your thoughts. Stop mid-sentence if you've been obsessing about what you could have/should have/would have done differently. Instead, change your chant to what you can't/won't/ shouldn't ever do or take in a relationship again. The point? When you check out what happened or what went wrong in a relationship, you can figure out how to try to make sure it doesn't go wrong again, or if it does, to at least (hopefully) recognize it when it's happening (or, you can just blame him).

Give yourself six weeks. According to studies, this is about how long it takes to get over a severe loss.

Vow NOT to swear off men. Research has found women who avoid any emotional attachment after a bad break-up are much more likely to leave or destroy their next relationship for fear of getting hurt again.

Wait at least **90 days** before having sex again (think of it as your ex-relationship's warranty). Apparently, researchers have found that this is enough time to let your body get charged up for sex again.

Send his stuff packing. Studies show that we get physically addicted to the pheromones secreted by the person we sleep with. So by cleaning the house, you're psychologically telling yourself that you are making room for something (or someone!) new.

Walk past a **construction site** once a day.

SOCIAL RUTS

Match your mood to your support system.

64

Visit your mother if you want to be babied and cooked your favourite foods.

Find your dad if you just want to hang out silently with someone and maybe hammer a few things.

35

66

Call your best friend when you need to hear how sexy, smart and wonderful you are.

Get together with a happily married couple if you need instant proof that being back with the 'singletons' is better.

67

68

Gather single girlfriends when you're ready to go prowling for fresh meat and **have catty bitch sessions** about your ex (they've been there, done it and bought the T-shirt).

69

Dial male friends when you need reminding that not all men are swine.

70

Look up **an old ex** for a passionate fling.

71

Get in touch with his friends when you need to let out all the venomous things you have ever felt about him. It should (a) get back to your ex and (b) allow you to gauge whether the listener likes or dislikes your ex, perhaps giving you something in common in case you wish to shoot for tip 25 with any of them.

EX HIM OUT

Exorcise your ex for good.

72

Go ahead and give in to your impulse to gab about him 24/7. A group of students at the University of Virginia were told to talk for ten minutes about any topic EXCEPT an old flame. After, when asked to think about their exes, their bodies showed high stress. Conclusion: you NEED to verbally agonize in order to heal.

Instead of seeing him as **Ex-Guy Love God**, change your mental image to Ex-Guy Anal Retentive, a mental, midget, control freak, who loses it if you have to work even an hour late.

73

Replace the photograph of him next to your bed with one of your precious pooch.

74

Make a list – yes one of THOSE – about everything that was bad about the relationship (be honest!). He nagged you. You didn't trust him. You didn't have a lot in common. You get the picture. Carry the list for the next few days to get you over the 'I want him back' hump. Refer to it as necessary.

Insert **'bastard'** (or some similar epitaph) every time you say or think his name.

76

Section Three

Anger

why does this have
to happen to me?

This is the 'Arrgh! I'm so mad I could spit' stage. Bitterness and regret rule as you obsess how you gave this man three good dates/months/years – time that could have been spent doing … well, other things. With other men! You're not sure with whom, but they would have been awesome. Instead, you were working like a dog to build something real and lasting with that (fill in appropriate noun). Well, if he thinks he can treat you like that, forget about it.

The thing about anger is that you need it for recovery – experts have found that a little outrage goes a long way towards stimulating adrenaline, making you feel stronger and more confident. The danger is that you can get so stuck in your 'he loses his hair/job/life' fantasies that you don't move on with your own life.

Don't fight your rage; feel the pain, but direct it. Here's how to get mad, get even and then get over him.

REVENGE IS SWEET

Make him pay without risk.

77

You may think you need to **trash him** to move on. But according to research, getting revenge is exactly what prevents you from moving on. Apparently, every second you waste focused on him is one second less that you are going to feel better. If you can't help yourself, see tips 80, 81 and 83 for how to do it without leaving a trace.

Write a hate letter to your ex. Then destroy it. Repeat as often as necessary.

Get together with your friends and, using a doll, hold a mock funeral for him. Or destroy his photo, slowly ripping it as if you were tearing out his heart.

80

If you must get him, **keep it legal**. Call and tell him you have an STD (this is a double whammy because he'll think you were cheating on him). Get him a personal ad, saying he prefers 'full-bodied,' older women. Report all his credit cards as stolen. Sign him up for every piece of free junk e-mail under the sun. If he doesn't change his phone security code (and who ever does?), check his messages and delete any important ones (translation: those from women and bosses).

Check out these ultimate revenge websites; they'll do all your evil work for you:

www.virtual-design.com/demos/voodoodoll
Design your own virtual voodoo doll to torture and e-mail him the gruesome playback.
www.flwyd.dhs.org/curse When you've run out of every four-letter word in your vocabulary, pick one from the Elizabethan Curse Generator.
www.anonymizer.com Send all the vicious stuff you want and NEVER get traced or found out.
www.dogdoo.com Get down and dirty and send him virtual doggie poo.
www.deathclock.com For true peace of mind you can find out when your ex's time on earth is up.

81

82

Plan your revenge in detail. Psychologists say that, for example, dreaming that you called his boss about him skimming money on his accounts so he gets fired without a reference, never gets another job, ends up homeless and alone, etc., is better than actually doing it. It reminds you that you have the power, girl. You just choose to use it only for good.

83

Use your pain and get creative. Alanis Morissette hit it big with her Grammy-winning song 'You Oughta Know' about getting dumped; Carly Simon grossed $2.5 million from her song about a vain ex-lover; Ivana Trump has made millions playing the trump card after The Donald left her for a younger model; and Mia Farrow received $3 million for trashing her life with Woody Allen, after he left her for her adopted daughter.

84

Know your local revenge laws; it could serve you well. In Singapore, a 32-year-old woman who made more than 60 crank calls a day to her ex's fiancée was fined almost £5,000 for harassment.

EX-FILES

Your manual for surviving sickeningly common close ex-encounters (no tissues required).

THE SITUATION: Arranging to return each other's personal stuff after the split.

DO: Make a list of everything that's yours and tell him he can do the same. If you don't think you can maintain your cool, get a friend to do the drop-off for you. Alternatively, arrange a blind drop-off in front of each other's homes.

DON'T: Meet at venues where you're likely to be flooded with nostalgic 'wasn't it wonderful' memories and either fall into a weeping heap or a sizzling snog for the trade-off. Also, don't bother with anything that's not valuable or has no sentimental value – replace it with a newer, better one.

THE SITUATION: The first post-break-up encounter.

86

DO: Accept that you're probably going to hate how you look, even if you look fabulous. Let HIM say the first sentence after the initial greetings. Then casually say you'd love to talk (this is key – otherwise it looks like you are avoiding him), but you have to meet someone. Saunter off straight to the nearest phone to call your closest friend, telling her in detail what he was wearing, what he said, how he said it, etc.

DON'T: Start crying, laughing hysterically, talking non-stop or mauling him.

SITUATION: Seeing him talking (or flirting!) with another woman.

DO: Give him a teensy smile (as in, 'Uh-huh, got your number, dude'), nod and walk, don't run, straight to the nearest phone … you know the drill.

DON'T: Approach him, find your own boy model to flirt with or collapse in a soppy, snivelling mess.

SITUATION: Meeting at a party and, 'accidentally' getting together.

DO: Accept that it happens. A lot. So don't dwell on it.

DON'T: Call him. What can you say to him that hasn't been said already? Think of it as your goodbye 'kiss'.

SITUATION: Bumping into him and his pretty new girlfriend.

DO: Smile. Be civil. Ask how he's doing. Say hi to the new babe. Then find that best friend. Unless, of course, you're with YOUR new guy. Who happens to look exactly like George Clooney (dream come true!). In which case, flaunt it.

DON'T: Be tempted to spill all the gory moments of your break-up to your new guy or his new girl. If either ask, just say, 'We used to go out.'

89

9 USES FOR AN EX-BOYFRIEND

Your relationship wasn't a total waste of time.

Comeback to your mum
When she gives her 'Why aren't you married like all your sisters and cousins' speech, simply say, 'Well you didn't want me to marry that last loser, did you?'

Wake-up call
Keep a picture of your ex to remind yourself that you should be dating men who didn't skip a link in the evolutionary chain.

92

Exercise incentive
You'd rather detour miles than risk running into him on his old turf.

Blame magnet
Make him the scapegoat for everything bad in your life – the backpack you can't find, the bad mood you're in, your addiction to KitKats.

93

Urge to splurge
Now you have the perfect excuse to toss out those old faded sheets.

94

95

Stress relief
Smash anything
he left behind to
smithereens.

Artistic inspiration
For your soon-to-be
critically acclaimed
work, entitled
'Ex Out'.

96

Wild sex

97

Getting smarter
Relationship psychologists say the best
thing an ex is good for is to figure out what
traits you DON'T want in a boyfriend.

98

Section Five

Acceptance

it happened and I'll live
to love again

OK, you're through to the final lap. You have acknowledged the plain fact that the relationship is over ('Whew, it's been six weeks since we ended it and I realized the other day I haven't thought about him for one whole day').

Most psychologists agree that during this process you learn to accept yourself and become ready to move on. You've vented your feelings, now it is time to go beyond merely surviving the heartbreak and figuring out how to avoid it in the future.

This means:
(1) Keeping a level head when it comes to dating;
(2) taking an emotional inventory so you know what you want and expect out of your next relationship (quick fling versus real thing); and,
(3) most importantly, having faith – even if you are a vile wicked witch, there is an equally vile warlock out there for you.

WRAP IT UP

You're finally over him when …

You genuinely hope he is happy when you hear he's with someone new.

You can go to what used to be your **favourite restaurant**, eat what used to be your favourite dish AND enjoy it.

He calls, saying he made a **big mistake** and wants you to come back, and you put him on hold to take a call from your mother.

You finally toss out all the love mementos – not because they cause you pain, but because you need the shelf space.

You compare **New Guy to Ex-Guy** and instead of thinking New Guy comes up short, you realize New Guy is a total upgrade from Ex-Guy ('Wow! Ex-Guy never gave me an hour-long back massage.' 'Huh! Ex-Guy never listened when I complained about work.' 'Mmm. Ex-Guy could never find my G-Spot.').

SINGLED OUT

Why it's great to be single (honest).

You can **flirt** with your (incredibly cute) local bartender without your guy shooting green laser beams into your back.

104

You don't have to **hang out** with your ex's slacker friend anymore (the one who thought playing air guitar was a talent).

105

You can spend the night drooling over **Brad Pitt** flicks without hearing a lot of snide remarks.

107

You can swap Rush Hour 2-meets-American Pie movies for **chick flicks without guilt**.

Did we mention **flirting** with your (incredibly cute) local bartender?

When you **have sex** with someone new, he doesn't wonder why you no longer want to do that kinky little thing he likes so much.

You get precious **alone-time**. In researching the effects of sensory deprivation, the ultimate solitude, Peter Suedfeld, PhD, a University of British Columbia psychologist who studies isolation, found that after just one hour of being totally on their own, people show lower blood pressure, higher mental functioning, enhanced creativity and a more positive outlook.

LOVER, COME BACK

Do you really want him back?

11 **Take two or three weeks to think** about restarting the connection. Suddenly being alone can feel terrible and alienating, and a lot of people have the knee-jerk reaction of wanting to make the loneliness go away by getting the other person back.

12 **Which of the following** thought processes best describes your current reality?
(a) It's not like I'm home every night sighing over him. It's been more than two weeks since we broke up. But I still dig him. And I can see where things went wrong and how we can work it out this time.
(b) Getting back together with my ex is better than being miserable and alone.
(c) I'm planning to dump his sorry ass the minute he takes me back.

It's (a) or nothing. Psychologists say if you have a life without your ex, but you've been thinking about your relationship and have realized that, uh, actually you still like him, you're thinking clearly. Ergo: your chances of staying together second time around are good. Any other answer means that you're still hurting. Get back together with him now, and you may never recover. And you'll probably kill a good deal of self-esteem as well.

3 If tip 112 holds true for you, then **go for it**. When Nancy Kalish, PhD, studied more than 500 couples that had called it quits, she found a surprising 72 per cent reunited and stayed together. The reason? They now had more realistic expectations of what they both wanted out of the relationship.

4 **But wait at least a year**. In the same study, Dr Kalish found that the longer a couple stayed apart, the more successful their reunion. Seems you need time to carve out your own identity and not be so-and-so's girlfriend for a while before you can truly decide if you WANT to be his arm jewellery again.

LOVE TURNAROUND

Caution: If he dumped you and is now creeping back, his reasons are not necessarily honourable.

He misses the sex. Hey, he's a man and he has needs! He wants his usual and customary style of loving with a partner he is familiar with. He feels safe with you and comfortable, because you know what he likes. But sex is not enough to keep a man – never has been and never will be. Things will deteriorate right back to square one because he is not there for the long haul, only a quick roll.

He needs to know you still care. In other words, he has seen you out on the town having a good time with some hot dude and needs to know he hasn't been replaced. His goal is to stay in contact with you and maintain your focus on him, just enough to keep the door open IN CASE he decides later that he wants to come back to you.

He doesn't want to start over. Thinking about the time he will need to spend trying to replace you is overwhelming. He thinks about the energy required to establish a foundation and framework for a new relationship and he gets a headache. He would rather apologize, give you what you want and just move on down the road with the woman who understands him and shares a history with him. Basically, he is lazy and would rather fight than switch.

He realizes he messed up bad. He has a chronic case of guilt. Now that he has had time away from you and the situation, he's come to the shocking realization that he truly cares for you (more than he knew). Don't keel over, it may be the dreaded 'L' word at work here! He has gone out, dated other women, hung out with his guy friends, and realized he isn't having the big fun he thought he would. His life is empty and meaningless without you in it. He is depressed, unmotivated, moody and very unhappy. He comes to you to get back together when he is willing to make the adjustments and apologies and changes needed to return the relationship to its former level of focus and commitment, and move forward in love. To demonstrate his seriousness, he may make promises of a future and offer homes, cars, trips *and* wedding rings. In short, go for it.

HAPPILY EVER AFTER

Your checklist for figuring out if it's time to get back in the love saddle.

119

If you **think about your ex at least once a day** (or are still having sex with him), would take your ex back in a heartbeat (even if you were dating someone else), have a crush on a man because he reminds you of your ex, still carry your ex's photo or feel like you are never going to be in love again, then you are in no way ready to jump-start your love life. Psychologists warn that if you starting to date before you've recovered from your old relationship, you could set up a situation where you man-hop in your search for eternal love. To stop the madness, do the drill in tip 58. Only when you understand what went wrong in the last relationship can you figure out how to avoid it again.

Consider your motives for wanting to date again. A love affair is not a cure-all for what ails you. Polls have found that the people who are happiest being in a relationship are the ones who are also happiest being on their own (see tip 110).

You are ready for new love when you can deal with **answering questions** about your last relationship without auto-crying, blaming him or ranting.

Bouncing back into a **new romance** can be a good cure for a broken heart. It dulls the pain, numbs the loss and revives your shattered self-esteem, but only if you slip into it with the right attitude. You should want to have fun, not a relationship.

Repeatedly ask yourself: **Would I want this guy for a friend?** Studies have found that the best post-break-up boyfriend is a man who reminds you of your male friends rather than of your ex. These are the guys you've always enjoyed hanging out with on a Saturday afternoon and whose values you share.